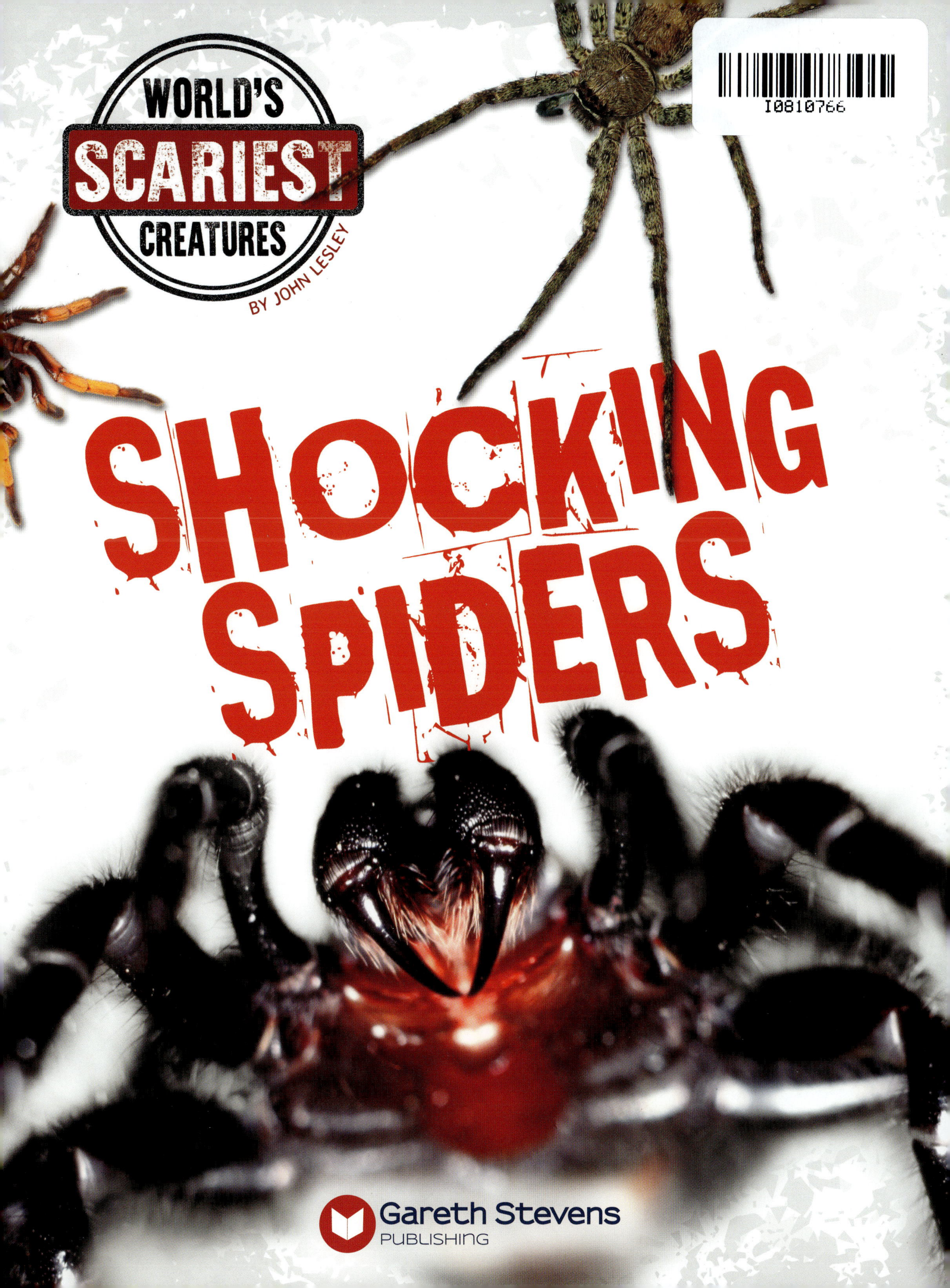

WORLD'S
SCARIEST
CREATURES
BY JOHN LESLEY
SHOCKING SPIDERS
Gareth Stevens
PUBLISHING

Please visit our website,
www.garethstevens.com.
For a free color catalog of all
our high-quality books, call
toll free 1-800-542-2595 or
fax 1-877-542-2596.

Cataloging-in-Publication Data
Names: Lesley, John.
Title: Shocking spiders / John Lesley.
Description: Buffalo, NY : Gareth Stevens Publishing, 2026. | Series: World's scariest creatures | Includes glossary and index.
Identifiers: ISBN 9781482474176 (pbk.) | ISBN 9781482474183 (library bound) | ISBN 9781482474190 (ebook)
Subjects: LCSH: Spiders--Juvenile literature.
Classification: LCC QL458.4 L475 2026 | DDC 595.4'4--dc23

Published in 2026 by
Gareth Stevens Publishing
2544 Clinton St.
Buffalo, NY 14224

First published 2025 by Redback Publishing

Author: John Lesley
Editor: Simone Saba
Designer: Redback Publishing
Original illustrations © Redback Publishing 2025
Originated by Redback Publishing

Acknowledgements
Abbreviations: l—left, r—right, b—bottom, t—top, c—centre, m—middle

We would like to thank the following for permission to reproduce photographs © Shutterstock; p10-11c Slow Walker/Shutterstock.com; p24tc Karla Quintana Pearce, CC BY 2.0 <https://creativecommons.org/licenses/by/2.0>, via Wikimedia Commons; p24mr JonRichfield, CC BY-SA 3.0 <https://creativecommons.org/licenses/by-sa/3.0>, via Wikimedia Commons; p25, 2ndtl Johan C.G. Fagerholm, CC BY-SA 3.0 <http://creativecommons.org/licenses/by-sa/3.0/>, via Wikimedia Commons; p25bl Rison Thumboor from Thrissur, India, CC BY 2.0 <https://creativecommons.org/licenses/by/2.0>, via Wikimedia Commons; p25br Judy Gallagher, CC BY 2.0 <https://creativecommons.org/licenses/by/2.0>, via Wikimedia Commons; p31tr Stu's Images, CC BY-SA 3.0 <https://creativecommons.org/licenses/by-sa/3.0>, via Wikimedia Commons

Printed in the United States of America

CPSIA compliance information: Batch #CSGS26
For further information contact Gareth Stevens at 1-800-542-2595.

CONTENTS

HUNTSMAN SPIDER

Sparassidae

Bigger than a hand, hairy and scary, huntsman spiders look terrifying, but they are not as dangerous as you might think. These are the spiders that often wander into houses and sit in the middle of a wall, looking menacing.

LIFE CYCLE

After mating, the female lays a few hundred eggs in a sac made of silk. She guards the eggs until they hatch, and may carry the egg sac around with her. The spiderlings molt out of their hard, outer skins many times as they grow.

HABITAT

Huntsman spiders are found in tropical, subtropical, and warm temperate regions. They are common in Australia, Africa, Asia, the Mediterranean Basin, and the Americas.

FACT

They often get into cars and scamper across the windshield!

FACT FILE

Width including legs: about 6 inches (15 cm)
Color: brown or gray
Venomous: yes
Habitat: narrow gaps in houses, bark on trees, or among rocks and leaf litter
Lifespan: around 2 years

FACT

Huntsman spiders sometimes live in groups with hundreds of other huntsman spiders!

FOOD

Huntsman spiders hunt and eat insects, small lizards, and other small creatures they can catch. They do not use a web but run after their prey and grab it.

PREDATORS

Predators of huntsman spiders include reptiles, spider wasps, birds, and people.

VENOM AND BITING

A huntsman spider bite and the venom it produces is not lethal to a healthy adult, but it will cause pain at the site of the bite. Huntsman spiders will run away rather than fight, but they will certainly bite if touched and threatened.

WOLF SPIDER

Lycosidae

Wolf spiders are big and may be covered in soft gray or brown hair that looks like fur. Some have stripes on their back. If you shine a flashlight onto your lawn at night and see lots of tiny eyes shining back at you, they may belong to wolf spiders out hunting.

LIFE CYCLE

After mating, the female lays her eggs in a silk sac and carries it around until they hatch. She then carries them on her back until they are big enough to fend for themselves. The spiderlings spread to new areas by spinning a thread of silk and using it to be blown away by the wind. This is called ballooning.

HABITAT

Wolf spiders are found worldwide, from the Arctic to the tropics. They are found on every continent except Antarctica. Some build deep burrows with doors, twigs, and stones to protect the entrance.

FOOD

Wolf spiders hunt and eat insects, frogs, and other small creatures. Their name comes from their habit of stalking their prey and then pouncing on it.

FACT

There may be wolf spiders living in your lawn right now!

FACT FILE

Body length: about 1.2 inches (3 cm)

Color: gray-brown hairy bodies with brown patterns

Venomous: yes

Habitat: across the world in burrows or among rocks and leaves on the ground

Lifespan: males, around one year; females, several years

PREDATORS

Creatures that eat wolf spiders include small mammals, reptiles, amphibians, birds, and larger spiders.

VENOM AND BITING

Wolf spider venom is not lethal to humans, unless they have an allergy to it. The bite site will be painful and swollen and may need medical attention.

SYDNEY FUNNEL-WEB SPIDER

Atrax robustus

The Sydney funnel-web spider is considered to be the deadliest spider in the world. Large and very aggressive, it lives just as happily in gardens as in wild areas. The female has a thicker body than the male, and both have large silk spinnerets at the end of the abdomen.

LIFE CYCLE

The males wander in search of a mate. After mating, a female usually kills the male she mates with. The female lays about 100 eggs in her burrow. After hatching, they leave to build their own burrows.

HABITAT

The funnel-web spider builds a silk-lined burrow among rocks, trash, or shoes left outside. It lays lines of silk around the entrance to trap prey. Its preferred environments are the moist, southeastern forests and gardens of Australia.

FOOD

The funnel-web spider eats insects, lizards, and frogs.

FACT FILE

Body length: about 1.2 inches (3 cm)
Color: shiny, black or dark brown
Venomous: yes
Habitat: in burrows in forests and gardens
Lifespan: perhaps over 10 years
People bitten and hospitalized each year: about 25

WARNING!

It's the deadliest spider in the world!

FACT

The male funnel-web spider can live under water for hours.

PREDATORS

Predators of funnel-web spiders include reptiles, spider wasps, and birds.

VENOM AND BITING

If you dig up a funnel-web burrow, the spider will rear up on its back legs, displaying its long fangs. It will then attack you, injecting venom that can be lethal to humans.

TRAPDOOR SPIDER

Arbanitis

Trapdoor spiders usually build burrows in the ground with a little round door made from silk and soil. They wait at the entrance until something to eat passes by. Then they grab it, inject venom, and eat it.

Trapdoor spiders have strong, stocky bodies and are often confused with funnel-web spiders. Trapdoors have smaller silk spinnerets than the funnel-web spider and are covered in hairs. These two features help to tell them apart.

LIFE CYCLE

Trapdoor spiders wander around when looking for a mate. The female lays eggs inside her own burrow. After hatching, the spiderlings leave and make their own tiny burrows.

HABITAT

Not all trapdoor spiders build burrows with doors. The burrow is different from that of a funnel-web spider as it does not have lines of silk around the entrance to trap prey. Trapdoor spiders live in moist areas around the eastern parts of Australia and in a few locations in the far southwest.

FACT

Trapdoor and funnel-web spiders look similar. Keep away from both!

FACT

Trapdoor spiders dig burrows that can be 16 inches (40 cm) deep!

FACT FILE

Body length: about 1.2 inches (3 cm)
Color: dark brown
Venomous: yes
Habitat: moist areas in the east or southwest of Australia
Lifespan: about 10 years

FOOD

As they live in burrows or on the ground, these spiders eat insects and bugs that they find there.

PREDATORS

Birds and wasps eat trapdoor spiders that have come out into the open.

VENOM AND BITING

Trapdoor spiders are not very aggressive but may stand up on their rear legs if threatened. Their venom is not known to be lethal to humans, although a bite can be very painful and cause swelling.

GOLIATH BIRDEATER SPIDER

Theraphosa blondi

The Goliath birdeater is the largest species of spider by weight in the world. They have a leg span that can reach up to 12 inches (30 cm).

LIFE CYCLE

After mating, the female lays her eggs in a large silk sac. She stays near the sac and guards it until the spiderlings hatch.

HABITAT

Goliath birdeaters prefer to live in humid, tropical rainforests and are found in northern South America.

FOOD

Despite their name, Goliath birdeaters rarely eat birds. They mainly eat insects, worms, and other arthropods, as well as small vertebrates like frogs, lizards, and occasionally small rodents or birds.

VENOM AND BITING

Their venom is not highly toxic to humans.

FACT

When threatened, Goliath birdeaters raise their front legs and can produce a hissing sound.

FACT FILE

Body length: about 4.75 inches (12 cm)

Color: hairy body that is usually brown to dark brown

Venomous: yes

Habitat: tropical rainforests in northern South America

REDBACK SPIDER

Latrodectus hasselti

FACT

Redback spiders like to hide in cabinets and behind furniture!

The bright red stripe down its black, shiny abdomen makes this spider instantly recognizable. It builds messy nests around and inside houses and in gardens. Their presence in outdoor toilets is legendary in the Australian outback.

LIFE CYCLE

The male redback spider is tiny compared to the female and it may not have a red mark on its body. It waits on the edge of her web for a chance to mate. The female egg sacs are about 0.4 inch (1 cm) wide and scattered throughout her web. After hatching, the spiderlings will eat each other. They disperse by ballooning, which involves making a long line of silk and blowing away with it in the wind.

HABITAT

It is found throughout most of Australia, particularly near buildings, where their numbers are often at pest level.

FACT

After, and even during, mating, the female starts to eat the tiny male!

FACT FILE

Female body length: about 0.4 inch (1 cm)
Color: shiny black with a red stripe
Venomous: yes
Habitat: in wild areas and around farms and houses
Lifespan: about 2 years for females
People bitten and hospitalized each year: about 280

FOOD

They mostly eat insects that stumble into their web.

VENOM AND BITING

The redback spider was once thought to be the most dangerous in Australia. Redback spiders stay in their web, which makes them less frightening for humans than other big spiders that like to wander.

BRAZILIAN WANDERING SPIDER

Phoneutria

The Brazilian wandering spider, sometimes called the banana spider or armed spider, is renowned for its potent venom and wandering behavior.

LIFE CYCLE

The female lays her eggs in a silk sac, which she guards until they hatch.

HABITAT

Brazilian wandering spiders are found in tropical regions of Central and South America.

FOOD

This spider eats insects and other spiders. It even catches and eats small vertebrates like frogs and lizards.

VENOM

The Brazilian wandering spider can be very aggressive when threatened. Their venom is very strong, it is one of the most potent venoms of any spider.

FACT

They have eight eyes arranged in three rows, providing good vision to detect prey and threats.

FACT FILE

Body length: about 1-2 inches (2.5-5 cm)

Color: brown to grayish-brown with distinctive dark bands on their legs

Venomous: yes

Habitat: tropical regions of Central and South America

RED-HEADED MOUSE SPIDER

Missulena

This spider has a sturdy, large body and enormous fangs. The female is larger than the male and is glossy dark brown or black. The male has a bright red head and a blue abdomen.

LIFE CYCLE

The males wander to find a female. After mating, the female lays eggs and makes an egg sac out of silk. The egg sac is placed in the burrow for protection. After hatching, the spiderlings use ballooning on silk threads to spread to new areas.

HABITAT

This spider lives in forests and dry wild areas. It is rarely near houses. They build burrows that are up to 1.6 feet (0.5 m) long, with trapdoors and a silk lining. The burrow is unusual in having a side passage where the spider can hide from any predator that gets into the main burrow.

FACT

The venom is as deadly as that of the funnel-web, but they may inject less of it.

FACT FILE

Female body length: up to 1.2 inches (3 cm)
Venomous: yes
Habitat: forests and wild areas
Lifespan: around 4 years

FACT

The name mouse spider comes from the fact that this spider digs a burrow like a mouse.

FOOD

Mouse spiders eat prey that they can catch on the ground, such as crawling insects, frogs, and bugs.

VENOM AND BITING

Although bites are rare, the effect of being bitten can be severe. Funnel-web spider antivenom is used for treatment.

BROWN RECLUSE SPIDER

Loxosceles reclusa

FACT

Brown recluses are shy and prefer to stay hidden and undisturbed.

The brown recluse spider is one of the most dangerous spiders in the world. A bite wound from this spider may take several months to heal. This spider is also called the violin spider because of the dark violin-shaped markings on their cephalothorax.

LIFE CYCLE

After mating in the warmer months, the female lays about 40 to 50 eggs in a silk sac. Brown recluse spiders typically live for two to four years.

HABITAT

Native to the central and southeastern United States, they prefer dark, secluded areas such as woodpiles, sheds, and under rocks. They also like basements, attics, closets, and to hide under furniture.

VENOM AND BITING

The venom of the brown recluse can cause necrotic skin lesions and systemic symptoms in humans.

FACT FILE

Body length: 0.25 to 0.75 inch (6 to 20 mm)

Color: light to dark brown

Venomous: yes

Habitat: central and southeastern United States

Lifespan: about 2 to 4 years

YELLOW SAC SPIDER

Cheiracanthium

The yellow sac spider is a small but dangerous spider known for its pale yellow color and the silk sac it makes to live in.

LIFE CYCLE

After mating, usually in the warmer months, a female yellow sac spider lays her eggs in a silk sac which she guards until they hatch. These spiders typically live for about one to two years.

HABITAT

Yellow sac spiders are found worldwide. They are highly adaptable and can be found in various habitats, including gardens, forests, and near people's homes.

FOOD

This spider feeds on insects and other small arthropods. They do not use webs to catch prey, relying on their speed and agility to hunt for food.

VENOM

While bites are not usually deadly to humans, they can cause pain, redness, and swelling, sometimes leading to a necrotic lesion similar to a mild brown recluse spider bite.

FACT

Yellow sac spiders have an elongated body with long, slender legs.

FACT FILE

Body length: from 0.2 to 0.4 inch (5 to 10 mm)

Color: usually pale yellow

Venomous: yes

Habitat: worldwide

WORLD'S MOST VENOMOUS SPIDERS

FEAR!

An intense fear of spiders is called arachnophobia. A low level of spider fear is common and probably a result of evolution.

GOLIATH BIRDEATER SPIDER

TRAPDOOR SPIDER, AUSTRALIA

QUESTION & ANSWER

What is the biggest spider in the world?

A: The Goliath birdeater spider from South America is the heaviest in the world, weighing up to 6.3 ounces (180 g), which is as heavy as a big orange!

The largest in size is the giant huntsman, with a width, including legs, of up to 1 foot (30 cm). They live in Laos.

GIANT HUNTSMAN SPIDER

FUNNEL-WEB SPIDER, AUSTRALIA

BLACK WIDOW SPIDER, NORTH AMERICA

FACT

A spider wasp digs a burrow then goes out and stings a spider. It drags the spider back into its burrow, lays an egg on it, and lets its larva feed on the spider.

BASIC SPIDER FACTS

They have eight legs.

LETHAL SPIDERS

Bites from highly toxic spiders can be fatal to humans. If you are bitten by a spider and are not sure if it is venomous, you should seek urgent medical attention as an antivenom may be necessary to save your life.

Spiders have been on Earth for about 400 million years.

Spiders are arachnids, which is a group of creatures that includes ticks, scorpions, and mites.

Altogether, spiders eat enormous quantities of insects around the world every day, helping to control insect numbers.

Spiders can regenerate lost legs.

The body has two parts: the cephalothorax and the abdomen.

The brain, stomach, and poison glands are located in the cephalothorax.

The lungs, heart, and reproductive organs are located in the abdomen.

SPIDER ADAPTATIONS

EYES

Spiders have many eyes, allowing them to see in many directions at once.

HAIR

The strong hairs on spider legs allow them to touch and find out what is around them. Hairs on the legs also taste and smell. Tufts of hairs on the ends of the legs help spiders to hang upside down on a smooth ceiling.

JUMPING SPIDER

FANGS

Spiders do not have teeth. They have fangs to inject venom, and hard parts in their mouth to hold onto food.

Spiders catch their food by hunting, using sticky webs, or waiting in a hidden spot until food comes to them.

VENOM

Spider venom stops prey from moving so that the spider can eat it. The venom does not always kill prey right away. It may just keep it alive but unable to escape until the spider is ready to eat it.

Another role for the venom is that it starts the digestion process so that the spider can suck up the body liquids instead of having to chew its prey.

SPIDER SILK

Spiders produce silk from spinnerets on their abdomen. The silk is used to construct webs and to wrap up food that they do not want to eat right away. The silk also keeps spider eggs safe.

FACT

Silk is extremely strong for something that is so thin. You will know this if you have ever walked into a web and had to pull it off yourself.

? QUESTION & ANSWER

Why don't spiders get stuck in their own webs?

A: Spiders that build webs produce a sticky silk for some parts, and a dry silk for others. The spider avoids walking on the sticky strands. It holds its body up off the web, walking using the claws on the tips of its legs.

GLOSSARY

Spider Word List

abdomen back part of a spider body

antivenom medicine used to treat a spider bite

ballooning producing a line of silk and using it to blow away in the wind

cephalothorax combined head and middle body of a spider

crevices narrow places

fang hollow mouthpart used to inject venom

lethal deadly

molt remove outer body covering

potent strong

prey animals that are eaten

sac pouch made of silk to hold spider eggs

scamper run quickly

spiderling juvenile spider

spinneret structures on the end of a spider abdomen for producing silk

toxic poisonous

venom poison produced by an animal for injection into prey or a predator

venomous having poison that is injected using fangs

INDEX